50 Moo-licious Recipes

By: Kelly Johnson

Table of Contents

- Creamy Cowboy Beef Stew
- Moo Moo Meatloaf Madness
- Juicy Lucy Stuffed Burgers
- Ranch Hand Ribeye Steak
- Dairy Dream Cheese Fondue
- Steakhouse Garlic Butter Bites
- Cheddar Chive Beef Sliders
- Smoky BBQ Brisket Burners
- Sirloin Sizzle Stir Fry
- Crispy Cowpoke Chicken Fried Steak
- Tenderloin Tango Tacos
- Moo-velous Meatball Subs
- Grilled Cowgirl Rib Tips
- Swiss Melt Philly Cheesesteak
- Chili Cow Casserole
- Blue Cheese Bacon Bombs
- Peppercorn Cowboy Steak Salad

- Creamy Cow's Mac & Cheese
- Beefy Bourbon Meatballs
- Heifer's Herb Roasted Roast
- Cowtipper Chimichurri Skewers
- Chuckwagon Chili Nachos
- Moo-licious Moussaka Magic
- Grass-Fed Beef Stir Fry
- Tender Cow Tacos Al Pastor
- Ribeye Ranch Wraps
- Moo Melt Grilled Cheese
- Sirloin & Spinach Stuffed Peppers
- Rustic Cowpoke Pot Roast
- BBQ Beef Burnt Ends
- The Cow's Creamy Stroganoff
- Seared Steak & Sweet Potato Bites
- Cowgirl's Cajun Beef Pasta
- Braised Beef & Root Veggies
- Beef & Bean Cowboy Chili
- Sizzlin' Saddle Steak Salad

- Grassfed Beef & Mushroom Pie
- Pepper Jack Beef Quesadilla
- Slow Cooker Sweet Cow Ribs
- Ribeye Ranchero Bowl
- The Mighty Moo Meat Pie
- Grilled Cowpoke Kabobs
- Creamy Cow Patty Soup
- Ground Beef Gyro Wraps
- Juicy Cowpoke Burger Bowl
- Rustic Ranch Beef & Barley
- Moo Melt Philly Rolls
- Herb Crusted Beef Tenderloin
- Classic Cowpoke Beef Stroganoff
- Smoky BBQ Beef Flatbread

Creamy Cowboy Beef Stew

Ingredients:

- Beef stew meat
- Onion, chopped
- Carrots, sliced
- Potatoes, diced
- Garlic, minced
- Beef broth
- Heavy cream
- Worcestershire sauce
- Flour or cornstarch (for thickening)
- Salt and pepper

Instructions:

1. Brown beef in a pot, then remove.
2. Sauté onions, garlic, carrots, and potatoes.
3. Return beef to pot, add broth and Worcestershire sauce, simmer until tender.
4. Stir in heavy cream and thicken with flour slurry if needed.
5. Season and serve hot.

Moo Moo Meatloaf Madness
Ingredients:

- Ground beef
- Bread crumbs
- Egg
- Onion, finely chopped
- Ketchup or BBQ sauce
- Worcestershire sauce
- Salt and pepper

Instructions:

1. Mix all ingredients except ketchup.
2. Shape into loaf and place in baking dish.
3. Spread ketchup or BBQ sauce on top.
4. Bake at 350°F until cooked through.
5. Let rest, slice, and serve.

Juicy Lucy Stuffed Burgers

Ingredients:

- Ground beef
- Cheese slices or cubes (cheddar or American)
- Salt and pepper
- Burger buns
- Toppings of choice

Instructions:

1. Divide beef into patties.
2. Place cheese between two patties and seal edges tightly.
3. Grill or pan-fry until cooked and cheese is melted inside.
4. Assemble burgers with buns and toppings.

Ranch Hand Ribeye Steak

Ingredients:

- Ribeye steaks
- Ranch seasoning mix
- Olive oil
- Salt and pepper

Instructions:

1. Rub steaks with olive oil and ranch seasoning.
2. Grill or pan-sear to desired doneness.
3. Rest steaks before slicing and serving.

Dairy Dream Cheese Fondue

Ingredients:

- Gruyère cheese, shredded
- Emmental cheese, shredded
- Garlic clove
- White wine
- Cornstarch
- Lemon juice
- Nutmeg

Instructions:

1. Rub pot with garlic.
2. Heat wine and lemon juice, slowly add cheese mixed with cornstarch.
3. Stir until melted and smooth.
4. Add a pinch of nutmeg.
5. Serve with bread cubes and veggies for dipping.

Steakhouse Garlic Butter Bites

Ingredients:

- Bread (baguette or French bread), sliced
- Butter, softened
- Garlic, minced
- Parsley, chopped
- Parmesan cheese (optional)

Instructions:

1. Mix butter, garlic, and parsley.
2. Spread on bread slices.
3. Sprinkle Parmesan if desired.
4. Toast in oven until golden and fragrant.

Cheddar Chive Beef Sliders

Ingredients:

- Ground beef
- Shredded cheddar cheese
- Fresh chives, chopped
- Slider buns
- Salt and pepper

Instructions:

1. Mix beef with chives, salt, and pepper.
2. Form small patties and cook to preferred doneness.
3. Add cheddar cheese on top to melt.
4. Serve on slider buns with your favorite toppings.

Smoky BBQ Brisket Burners

Ingredients:

- Smoked or cooked brisket, shredded
- BBQ sauce
- Slider buns or rolls
- Pickles (optional)

Instructions:

1. Warm shredded brisket with BBQ sauce.
2. Pile onto buns.
3. Add pickles if desired.
4. Serve immediately.

Sirloin Sizzle Stir Fry

Ingredients:

- Sirloin steak, thinly sliced
- Bell peppers, sliced
- Onion, sliced
- Garlic, minced
- Soy sauce
- Sesame oil
- Fresh ginger, grated
- Green onions (for garnish)

Instructions:

1. Heat sesame oil in a wok or skillet.
2. Stir-fry garlic and ginger briefly.
3. Add sirloin slices, cook until browned.
4. Toss in veggies and soy sauce, cook until tender-crisp.
5. Garnish with green onions and serve over rice or noodles.

Crispy Cowpoke Chicken Fried Steak

Ingredients:

- Cube steak
- Flour
- Salt and pepper
- Garlic powder
- Eggs
- Milk
- Oil for frying

Instructions:

1. Season flour with salt, pepper, and garlic powder.
2. Dip steak in egg and milk mixture, then dredge in seasoned flour.
3. Fry in hot oil until golden and cooked through.
4. Drain on paper towels and serve with gravy or your favorite sides.

Tenderloin Tango Tacos
Ingredients:

- Beef tenderloin, thinly sliced
- Taco seasoning
- Tortillas
- Fresh cilantro
- Diced onions
- Lime wedges
- Salsa or hot sauce

Instructions:

1. Season and sauté tenderloin until just cooked.
2. Warm tortillas.
3. Assemble tacos with beef, cilantro, onions, and salsa.
4. Serve with lime wedges.

Moo-velous Meatball Subs

Ingredients:

- Ground beef
- Breadcrumbs
- Egg
- Parmesan cheese
- Italian seasoning
- Marinara sauce
- Sub rolls
- Mozzarella cheese

Instructions:

1. Mix beef, breadcrumbs, egg, Parmesan, and seasoning.
2. Form meatballs and bake or pan-fry until cooked.
3. Heat meatballs in marinara sauce.
4. Place meatballs in rolls, top with mozzarella, and toast until cheese melts.

Grilled Cowgirl Rib Tips

Ingredients:

- Pork rib tips
- BBQ rub or seasoning
- BBQ sauce

Instructions:

1. Season rib tips with rub.
2. Grill over medium heat until tender and caramelized.
3. Brush with BBQ sauce during last few minutes.
4. Serve with extra sauce on the side.

Swiss Melt Philly Cheesesteak

Ingredients:

- Thinly sliced beef (ribeye or sirloin)
- Onions, caramelized
- Green peppers, sautéed
- Swiss cheese
- Hoagie rolls

Instructions:

1. Cook beef slices in skillet until browned.
2. Add onions and peppers until softened.
3. Layer beef and veggies with Swiss cheese on rolls.
4. Toast or broil until cheese melts.

Chili Cow Casserole

Ingredients:

- Ground beef
- Chili seasoning
- Beans (black or kidney)
- Diced tomatoes
- Corn
- Shredded cheese
- Tortilla chips (optional)

Instructions:

1. Brown beef and drain fat.
2. Add chili seasoning, beans, tomatoes, and corn.
3. Simmer until flavors meld.
4. Pour into casserole dish, top with cheese and crushed tortilla chips.
5. Bake until cheese is melted and bubbly.

Blue Cheese Bacon Bombs

Ingredients:

- Ground beef
- Blue cheese crumbles
- Cooked bacon strips
- Onion powder
- Garlic powder
- Salt and pepper

Instructions:

1. Mix beef with seasoning.
2. Form small patties, place blue cheese and bacon inside, then seal.
3. Grill or bake until cooked through and cheese is melted.
4. Serve as sliders or appetizers.

Peppercorn Cowboy Steak Salad

Ingredients:

- Grilled steak, sliced
- Mixed greens
- Cherry tomatoes
- Red onion, thinly sliced
- Crumbled blue cheese or feta
- Peppercorn dressing (olive oil, crushed peppercorns, vinegar, mustard)

Instructions:

1. Grill steak to preferred doneness and slice thinly.
2. Toss greens, tomatoes, and onions in a bowl.
3. Add steak slices and cheese on top.
4. Drizzle with peppercorn dressing and serve.

Creamy Cow's Mac & Cheese
Ingredients:

- Elbow macaroni
- Butter
- Flour
- Milk
- Cheddar cheese, shredded
- Parmesan cheese
- Salt and pepper

Instructions:

1. Cook macaroni and drain.
2. Make a roux with butter and flour, slowly whisk in milk to thicken.
3. Stir in cheeses until melted.
4. Mix cheese sauce with macaroni, season, and serve creamy.

Beefy Bourbon Meatballs

Ingredients:

- Ground beef
- Breadcrumbs
- Egg
- Bourbon
- Onion, finely chopped
- Garlic
- BBQ sauce

Instructions:

1. Mix beef, breadcrumbs, egg, onion, and garlic.
2. Form meatballs and brown in skillet.
3. Add bourbon and BBQ sauce, simmer until cooked through and sauce thickens.
4. Serve with toothpicks or over rice.

Heifer's Herb Roasted Roast

Ingredients:

- Beef roast
- Garlic
- Fresh rosemary and thyme
- Olive oil
- Salt and pepper

Instructions:

1. Rub roast with olive oil, garlic, herbs, salt, and pepper.
2. Roast in oven at 325°F until desired doneness.
3. Let rest before slicing.
4. Serve with pan juices or gravy.

Cowtipper Chimichurri Skewers

Ingredients:

- Beef cubes
- Chimichurri sauce (parsley, garlic, oregano, vinegar, oil)
- Skewers

Instructions:

1. Marinate beef cubes in chimichurri for at least an hour.
2. Thread onto skewers.
3. Grill to preferred doneness.
4. Serve with extra chimichurri on the side.

Chuckwagon Chili Nachos

Ingredients:

- Tortilla chips
- Chili (ground beef, beans, tomatoes, spices)
- Shredded cheese
- Jalapeños
- Sour cream
- Green onions

Instructions:

1. Spread tortilla chips on a baking sheet.
2. Top with chili and cheese.
3. Bake until cheese melts.
4. Garnish with jalapeños, sour cream, and green onions.

Moo-licious Moussaka Magic
Ingredients:

- Ground beef or lamb
- Eggplant, sliced and roasted
- Tomato sauce
- Onions and garlic
- Bechamel sauce (butter, flour, milk)
- Parmesan cheese

Instructions:

1. Cook beef with onions, garlic, and tomato sauce.
2. Layer roasted eggplant, meat sauce, and béchamel in a casserole dish.
3. Top with Parmesan.
4. Bake until golden and bubbly.

Grass-Fed Beef Stir Fry

Ingredients:

- Grass-fed beef strips
- Broccoli
- Bell peppers
- Soy sauce
- Garlic and ginger
- Sesame oil

Instructions:

1. Heat sesame oil in wok, add garlic and ginger.
2. Stir-fry beef until browned.
3. Add vegetables and soy sauce, cook until crisp-tender.
4. Serve with steamed rice.

Tender Cow Tacos Al Pastor
Ingredients:

- Thinly sliced beef or pork
- Pineapple chunks
- Al pastor seasoning or marinade
- Corn tortillas
- Cilantro and onions
- Lime wedges

Instructions:

1. Marinate meat in al pastor seasoning.
2. Grill or sauté with pineapple until caramelized.
3. Warm tortillas and fill with meat mixture.
4. Top with cilantro, onions, and squeeze lime.

Ribeye Ranch Wraps

Ingredients:

- Ribeye steak, thinly sliced
- Flour tortillas
- Lettuce
- Tomato slices
- Ranch dressing
- Shredded cheese

Instructions:

1. Cook ribeye slices to desired doneness.
2. Warm tortillas and spread ranch dressing.
3. Layer steak, lettuce, tomato, and cheese.
4. Roll tightly and slice in half to serve.

Moo Melt Grilled Cheese

Ingredients:

- Thick bread slices
- Cheddar cheese
- Sliced roast beef or deli beef
- Butter

Instructions:

1. Butter one side of each bread slice.
2. Layer cheese and beef between unbuttered sides.
3. Grill on medium heat until bread is golden and cheese melted.
4. Serve warm.

Sirloin & Spinach Stuffed Peppers

Ingredients:

- Bell peppers, halved and seeded
- Ground sirloin
- Fresh spinach, chopped
- Onion, diced
- Garlic, minced
- Tomato sauce
- Shredded cheese

Instructions:

1. Cook sirloin with onion and garlic until browned.
2. Stir in spinach and tomato sauce, cook until spinach wilts.
3. Stuff peppers with beef mixture, top with cheese.
4. Bake at 375°F until peppers soften and cheese bubbles.

Rustic Cowpoke Pot Roast

Ingredients:

- Beef chuck roast
- Carrots, chopped
- Potatoes, chopped
- Onion, quartered
- Beef broth
- Garlic
- Fresh thyme and rosemary

Instructions:

1. Sear roast in a pot, remove.
2. Sauté veggies briefly.
3. Add roast back with broth and herbs.
4. Cover and slow-cook until tender (oven or slow cooker).
5. Serve with veggies and pan juices.

BBQ Beef Burnt Ends

Ingredients:

- Beef brisket point, cubed
- BBQ rub
- BBQ sauce

Instructions:

1. Season brisket cubes with rub.
2. Smoke or slow-cook until tender.
3. Toss in BBQ sauce and cook a bit longer to caramelize.
4. Serve as a snack or main dish.

The Cow's Creamy Stroganoff

Ingredients:

- Sirloin strips
- Mushrooms, sliced
- Onion, diced
- Sour cream
- Beef broth
- Egg noodles
- Butter and flour (for roux)

Instructions:

1. Sauté beef strips until browned, remove.
2. Cook onions and mushrooms in butter.
3. Stir in flour, then broth to make sauce.
4. Return beef, simmer, and stir in sour cream.
5. Serve over cooked egg noodles.

Seared Steak & Sweet Potato Bites

Ingredients:

- Steak, cut into bite-sized pieces
- Sweet potatoes, diced
- Olive oil
- Garlic powder
- Fresh parsley

Instructions:

1. Roast sweet potatoes tossed with oil and garlic powder until tender.
2. Sear steak bites in a hot pan until browned.
3. Combine and garnish with parsley.
4. Serve as a hearty appetizer or side.

Cowgirl's Cajun Beef Pasta
Ingredients:

- Ground beef
- Cajun seasoning
- Bell peppers, sliced
- Onion, sliced
- Garlic, minced
- Penne pasta
- Heavy cream
- Parmesan cheese

Instructions:

1. Cook pasta and drain.
2. Sauté beef with Cajun seasoning, add veggies and garlic.
3. Stir in cream and Parmesan until sauce thickens.
4. Toss pasta with sauce and serve.

Braised Beef & Root Veggies

Ingredients:

- Beef chuck or brisket
- Carrots, parsnips, turnips, diced
- Onion
- Garlic
- Beef broth
- Thyme and bay leaves

Instructions:

1. Brown beef, then remove.
2. Sauté onions and garlic, add root veggies.
3. Return beef to pot with broth and herbs.
4. Cover and braise until beef is tender and veggies soft.
5. Serve warm with crusty bread.

Beef & Bean Cowboy Chili

Ingredients:

- Ground beef
- Kidney beans
- Black beans
- Diced tomatoes
- Onion, chopped
- Garlic, minced
- Chili powder
- Cumin
- Paprika
- Beef broth

Instructions:

1. Brown beef with onion and garlic.
2. Add spices, beans, tomatoes, and broth.
3. Simmer for at least an hour until flavors meld.
4. Serve hot with your favorite chili toppings.

Sizzlin' Saddle Steak Salad

Ingredients:

- Grilled steak strips
- Mixed greens
- Cherry tomatoes
- Red onion slices
- Avocado
- Balsamic vinaigrette

Instructions:

1. Grill steak and slice thinly.
2. Toss greens with veggies and avocado.
3. Top with steak strips and drizzle vinaigrette.
4. Serve immediately.

Grassfed Beef & Mushroom Pie

Ingredients:

- Ground grass-fed beef
- Mushrooms, sliced
- Onion, diced
- Garlic, minced
- Beef broth
- Flour (for thickening)
- Pie crust

Instructions:

1. Brown beef with onions and garlic.
2. Add mushrooms and cook until soft.
3. Stir in broth and thicken with flour.
4. Pour mixture into pie crust, cover with top crust.
5. Bake at 375°F until golden.

Pepper Jack Beef Quesadilla

Ingredients:

- Ground beef
- Pepper Jack cheese, shredded
- Flour tortillas
- Onion, diced
- Bell pepper, diced
- Taco seasoning

Instructions:

1. Cook beef with onions, peppers, and seasoning.
2. Place beef mixture and cheese on tortilla, top with another tortilla.
3. Cook in a skillet until cheese melts and tortillas are golden.
4. Slice and serve with salsa or sour cream.

Slow Cooker Sweet Cow Ribs

Ingredients:

- Beef ribs
- Brown sugar
- BBQ sauce
- Garlic powder
- Paprika
- Salt and pepper

Instructions:

1. Season ribs with spices and brown sugar.
2. Place in slow cooker, coat with BBQ sauce.
3. Cook on low for 6-8 hours until tender.
4. Finish on grill or broiler for a caramelized crust.

Ribeye Ranchero Bowl

Ingredients:

- Ribeye steak, grilled and sliced
- Cilantro lime rice
- Black beans
- Corn salsa
- Avocado slices
- Ranchero sauce

Instructions:

1. Grill steak and slice.
2. Assemble bowl with rice, beans, corn salsa, and avocado.
3. Top with steak and drizzle ranchero sauce.
4. Serve warm.

The Mighty Moo Meat Pie

Ingredients:

- Ground beef
- Onion, diced
- Garlic, minced
- Mixed vegetables (peas, carrots)
- Beef gravy
- Pie crust

Instructions:

1. Cook beef with onion and garlic.
2. Add vegetables and gravy, simmer.
3. Fill pie crust, top with second crust.
4. Bake at 375°F until golden and bubbly.

Grilled Cowpoke Kabobs

Ingredients:

- Beef cubes (sirloin or ribeye)
- Bell peppers
- Onion chunks
- Zucchini slices
- Marinade (olive oil, garlic, herbs, lemon juice)

Instructions:

1. Marinate beef and veggies for at least 30 minutes.
2. Thread onto skewers alternating beef and vegetables.
3. Grill until beef is cooked to liking and veggies are tender.
4. Serve hot.

Creamy Cow Patty Soup

Ingredients:

- Ground beef
- Onion, diced
- Carrots, chopped
- Celery, chopped
- Potatoes, diced
- Beef broth
- Heavy cream
- Flour (for thickening)
- Butter
- Salt and pepper

Instructions:

1. Brown ground beef in a large pot, drain excess fat.
2. Add onions, carrots, and celery; sauté until softened.
3. Stir in flour and butter to create a roux.
4. Slowly whisk in beef broth and bring to a simmer.
5. Add potatoes and cook until tender.
6. Stir in cream, season with salt and pepper, and warm through.
7. Serve hot with crusty bread.

Ground Beef Gyro Wraps

Ingredients:

- Ground beef
- Garlic powder
- Onion powder
- Dried oregano
- Ground cumin
- Salt and pepper
- Pita bread
- Tzatziki sauce
- Sliced tomatoes
- Red onion slices
- Lettuce

Instructions:

1. Season ground beef with spices and cook until browned.
2. Warm pita breads.
3. Assemble wraps with beef, tzatziki, tomatoes, onions, and lettuce.
4. Fold and serve.

Juicy Cowpoke Burger Bowl
Ingredients:

- Ground beef patties
- Mixed greens
- Cherry tomatoes
- Pickles
- Red onion slices
- Cheddar cheese, shredded
- Ranch or BBQ dressing

Instructions:

1. Grill or pan-fry beef patties to preferred doneness.
2. Assemble bowl with greens, tomatoes, pickles, onions, and cheese.
3. Top with sliced burger patties and drizzle dressing.
4. Serve immediately.

Rustic Ranch Beef & Barley

Ingredients:

- Stewing beef cubes
- Barley
- Carrots, diced
- Celery, diced
- Onion, diced
- Garlic, minced
- Beef broth
- Thyme and bay leaves

Instructions:

1. Brown beef cubes in a pot.
2. Add veggies and garlic; sauté briefly.
3. Add barley, broth, and herbs.
4. Simmer gently until beef and barley are tender.
5. Season to taste and serve warm.

Moo Melt Philly Rolls

Ingredients:

- Thinly sliced beef (sirloin or ribeye)
- Bell peppers, sliced
- Onions, sliced
- Provolone cheese slices
- Refrigerated crescent roll dough

Instructions:

1. Sauté beef, peppers, and onions until cooked.
2. Roll out crescent dough and layer with beef mixture and cheese.
3. Roll up and bake per dough instructions until golden and bubbly.
4. Slice and serve warm.

Herb Crusted Beef Tenderloin

Ingredients:

- Beef tenderloin roast
- Fresh rosemary and thyme
- Garlic, minced
- Olive oil
- Salt and pepper

Instructions:

1. Preheat oven to 400°F.
2. Rub tenderloin with olive oil, garlic, herbs, salt, and pepper.
3. Roast until desired doneness (medium-rare recommended).
4. Rest before slicing and serving.

Classic Cowpoke Beef Stroganoff

Ingredients:

- Beef strips (sirloin or tenderloin)
- Mushrooms, sliced
- Onion, diced
- Garlic, minced
- Sour cream
- Beef broth
- Flour and butter (for roux)
- Egg noodles

Instructions:

1. Brown beef strips; remove from pan.
2. Cook onions and mushrooms in butter.
3. Stir in flour, then broth to make sauce.
4. Return beef to pan, simmer, then stir in sour cream.
5. Serve over cooked egg noodles.

Smoky BBQ Beef Flatbread

Ingredients:

- Prepared flatbread or pizza crust
- Cooked shredded beef
- BBQ sauce
- Red onions, thinly sliced
- Mozzarella cheese
- Cilantro, chopped (optional)

Instructions:

1. Preheat oven to 425°F.
2. Spread BBQ sauce over flatbread.
3. Top with shredded beef, onions, and cheese.
4. Bake until cheese melts and crust is crispy.
5. Garnish with cilantro and slice to serve.